I0797321

Hamlet

Lightbox Literature Studies

John Perritano and Katie Gillespie

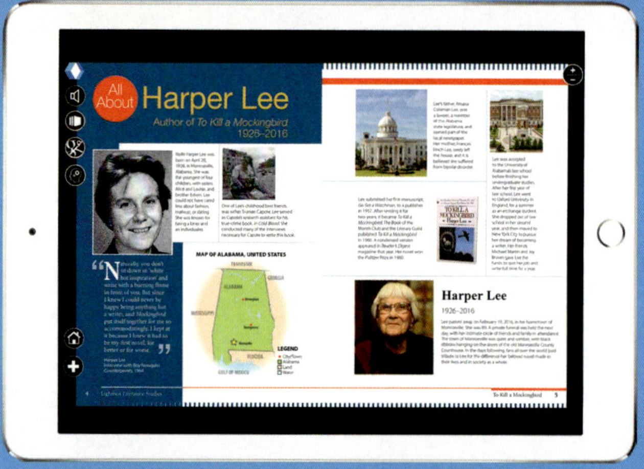

Lightbox is an all-inclusive digital solution for the teaching and learning of curriculum topics in an original, groundbreaking way. Lightbox is based on National Curriculum Standards.

STANDARD FEATURES OF LIGHTBOX

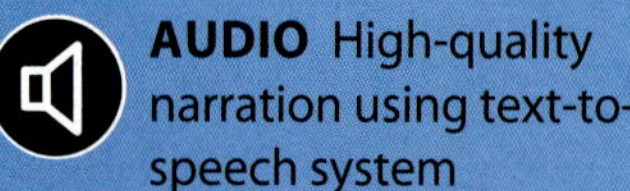

AUDIO High-quality narration using text-to-speech system

WEBLINKS Curated links to external, child-safe resources

INTERACTIVE MAPS Interactive maps and aerial satellite imagery

VIDEOS Embedded high-definition video clips

SLIDESHOWS Pictorial overviews of key concepts

QUIZZES Ten multiple choice questions that are automatically graded and emailed for teacher assessment

ACTIVITIES Printable PDFs that can be emailed and graded

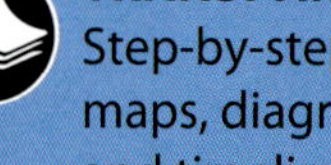

TRANSPARENCIES Step-by-step layering of maps, diagrams, charts, and timelines

KEY WORDS Matching key concepts to their definitions

MORE Extra information and details on the subject

FIRST HAND Letters, diaries, and other primary sources

DOCS Speeches, newspaper articles, and other historical documents

Contents

RUBRIC

Conducting an Interview

Students will conduct an interview with a community member about a time period in their community's history, and submit an audio recording and transcript of the interview. An exemplary interview will meet the following criteria.

- Clearly defines the purpose of the interview
- Conducts thorough background research to inform the focus of the interview and the questions
- Drafts a complete list of thoughtful, in-depth, and varied questions prior to the interview
- Interviews a subject with relevant knowledge on the topic and time period in question
- Asks questions in a logical order, building upon each other
- Treats the interview subject in a polite, respectful, and professional manner
- Does not interrupt or rush the interview subject
- Shows interest and enthusiasm in responses and follow-up questions
- Chooses follow-up questions that demonstrate active listening
- Asks for clarification and further details when necessary
- Asks questions about personal experiences related to the topic
- Asks questions regarding factual information and the interview subject's opinion on the topic
- Asks creative questions that reflect fresh insights on the topic
- Records the full interview in a quiet environment
- Organizes and edits the interview transcript to be clear and factual

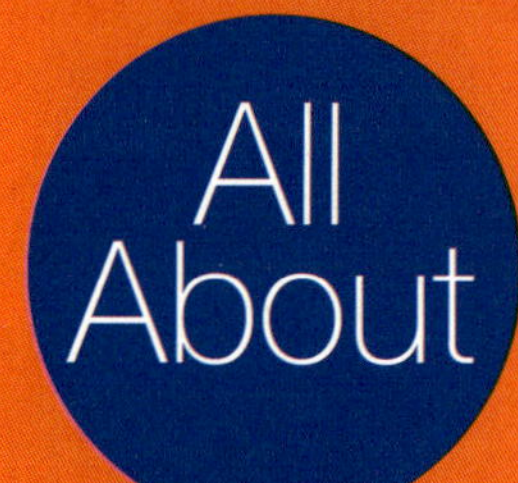

William Shakespeare

Author of *Hamlet*
1564–1616

William Shakespeare was born in Stratford, England, in 1564. His father, John, was 20 years old when he moved to Stratford from nearby Snitterfield. John Shakespeare immediately began working as a glove-maker, and was apparently successful because he purchased a house on Henley Street—William Shakespeare's birthplace. The elder Shakespeare became a prominent member of Stratford society. Records from Holy Trinity Church say that William Shakespeare was baptized on April 26, 1564, although there seems to be no record of his birth, and not much is known about his early life.

> "To be a well-favoured man is the gift of fortune; but to write and read comes by nature."
>
> Dogberry, *Much Ado About Nothing* by William Shakespeare, Act 3, Scene 3, Circa 1598

MAP OF THE UNITED KINGDOM

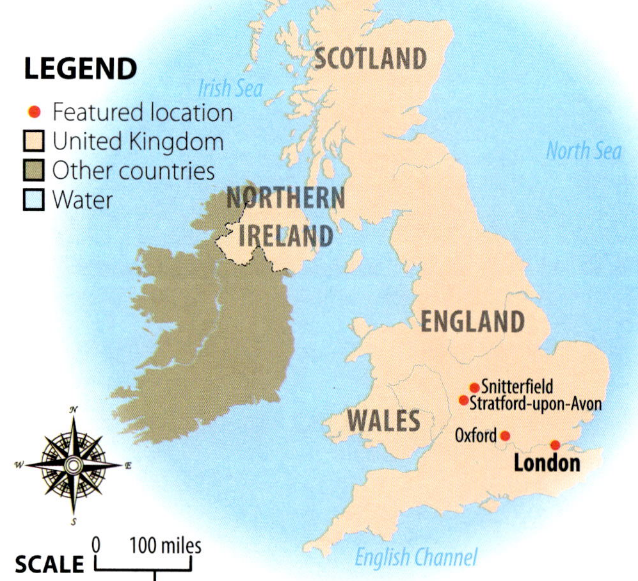

Although no records exist, most scholars surmise that Shakespeare attended school in Stratford. At the time, 15- or 16-year-old children from wealthy families often went on to Oxford or Cambridge after leaving grammar school, though Shakespeare never did. His father's fortunes worsened, so historians say it is reasonable to assume Shakespeare had to work to help pay the bills.

On November 28, 1582, the Bishop of Winchester granted Shakespeare a special **dispensation** to marry a woman named Anne Hathaway. Six months later, their first child, Susanna, was baptized in Holy Trinity Church. The pair would have three children. Eventually, the family relocated to London, where Shakespeare began working as an actor and playwright. By 1592, he is thought to have completed the *Wars of the Roses* plays and *The Two Gentlemen of Verona*.

According to scholars, Shakespeare began working as a cast member of Lord Chamberlain's company of actors, also known as the King's Men, around 1594. The company played in the famed Globe Theatre after its construction was completed in 1599. Not only was Shakespeare an actor and a playwright for the company, he was also a **shareholder**.

During his professional career, fellow playwrights, critics, and theatergoers liked to gossip about Shakespeare. Whatever they might have thought about him personally, there was no denying that his plays were entertaining. Many of them also served as **proverbs** called sententia, moral stories that stood separate from the play. Shakespeare died at the age of 52 on April 23, 1616.

ACTIVITIES

Google Maps

Kronborg Castle, Denmark

Explore the castle the inspired Shakespeare's Elsinore Castle, using street view.

First Hand

Interview: David Tennant on Hamlet

Examine this interview by Abigail Rokison from the University of Cambridge with actor David Tennant.

1. What types of questions does the interviewer ask? What topics does she focus on? Why would she focus on these specific areas?
2. Hamlet's madness is a popular topic of debate. When asked about his stance, Tennant says that "Whether or not he is mad is for the audience...to decide," an opinion that influenced his performance of the character. Do you think Shakespeare would agree with Tennant? Why or why not? In your opinion, is Hamlet's madness real or feigned? Cite examples from the play to support your position.

RUBRIC

Researching for a Writing Assignment

Students will complete a thorough research process to prepare for a writing assignment, and organize their research in a logical manner that supports their writing. An exemplary research process will meet the following criteria.

- Creates a goal for the research, based on the topic and working thesis
- Creates specific, thoughtful, and inventive research questions that are relevant to the topic of the writing assignment
- Produces a list of categories, key words, and related ideas to effectively assist in researching
- Uses high-quality sources that pertain to the topic and come in a variety of formats, such as books, journals, primary sources, websites, and databases
- Determines accuracy of all sources
- Uses sources that provide balanced research and various perspectives on the topic in question
- Takes notes to highlight the key facts and ideas in order to answer all research questions
- Extracts relevant, detailed information from the sources during the note-taking process
- Organizes the research notes in a clear and concise manner
- Organizes the research notes logically and in a way that sets up the information and ideas for analysis and the writing process
- Analyzes the information and produces ideas and points to support the working thesis
- Uses an effective and suitable format to present all research
- Properly cites all sources used

Setting of the Play

Hamlet is a tale of palace intrigue, revenge, distracted love, and murder. The play opens in the darkness and brutal cold of winter among the ramparts of Elsinore Castle in Denmark. Most of the action takes place between the brooding walls of the fortress. Tension is high as Prince Fortinbras of Norway, whose father was slain by King Hamlet, has risen up against Denmark, placing the guards at Elsinore on high alert.

Snapshot

1600–1601
The time period in which Shakespeare wrote ***Hamlet***.

1603
The year *Hamlet* **was published**.

4,024
The **number of lines** in *Hamlet*, the **longest** of any of Shakespeare's plays.

A Villain in Denmark

Ghost: "Taint not thy mind, nor let thy soul contrive
Against thy mother aught. Leave her to heaven,
And to those thorns that in her bosom lodge,
To prick and sting her. Fare thee well at once.
The glow-worm shows the matin to be near,
And 'gins to pale his uneffectual fire:
Adieu, adieu, adieu. Remember me."
Hamlet: "O all you host of heaven! O earth! What else?
And shall I couple hell? O, fie! Hold, hold, my heart;
And you, my sinews, grow not instant old,
But bear me stiffly up. Remember thee?
Ay, thou poor ghost, while memory holds a seat
In this distracted globe. Remember thee?
Yea, from the table of my memory
I'll wipe away all trivial fond records,
All saws of books, all forms, all pressures past,
That youth and observation copied there;
And thy commandment all alone shall live
Within the book and volume of my brain,
Unmix'd with baser matter. Yes, by heaven!
O most pernicious woman!
O villain, villain, smiling, damned villain!
My tables—meet it is I set it down
That one may smile, and smile, and be a villain;
At least I'm sure it may be so in Denmark."

Ghost and Hamlet, Act 1, Scene 5

However, Elsinore Castle was not conjured in the mind of Shakespeare. It is based on a real place, known as Kronborg Castle, and is currently a UNESCO World Heritage Site. Located on the northeastern tip of Zealand Island, a strategically important site overlooking the narrow Sound between Denmark and Sweden, the castle played an enormous role in European history between the sixteenth and eighteenth centuries. The location on which the castle stands has long had military significance. King Eric VII knew the strategic importance of the site in the 1420s and built a stronghold there.

During the time of Shakespeare, Denmark had a reputation for intrigue and war. The protestant movement began in the 1520s, leading to civil unrest and conflict throughout the country. Following the death of King Frederick I in 1534, a war of succession broke out. Two years later, the war was over, with the new king, Christian III, establishing the Danish Lutheran Church shortly thereafter.

ACTIVITIES

Video

Ghosts, Murder, and More Murder - Hamlet Part I: Crash Course Literature 203

Find out more about *Hamlet* by watching this video.

1. Why was Denmark chosen as the setting for this story? How do you think the play would be different if it were set in another country? Why?
2. In the video, John Green suggests that *Hamlet* is not really about Denmark, but is actually a commentary on Elizabethan England. Who might this commentary have been directed at and why? What messages could Shakespeare have been trying to convey? How successful was he in doing so?

Weblink

Claudius and the Condition of Denmark

Learn more about the conditions of Denmark in Shakespeare's *Hamlet*.

1. In the essay, Alexander W. Crawford claims that the weakness and corruption of Denmark under Claudius allow for the warlike activities of Fortinbras. Do you agree with this assessment? Why or why not?
2. Crawford says that Hamlet is the only character who understands the truth about what is happening in Denmark. Why do you think this is the case? Give evidence to support your answer.

RUBRIC

Analyzing a Video

Students will watch and assess a video related to a component of the play, and write an analysis of the video. An exemplary video analysis will meet the following criteria.

- Identifies the purpose of the video
- Identifies the intended audience of the video
- Describes how the content of the video is presented
- Summarizes the information and opinions presented in the video
- Analyzes the quality of the content presented in the video
- Assesses the effectiveness of the video
- Discusses the technical aspects of the video and whether or not these enhance the content
- Determines whether the images and graphics used in the video relate to the content
- Determines whether the video is easy to follow and understand
- Gives the analysis a clear and consistent purpose
- Organizes the analysis in a logical, effective manner
- Presents a strong, clear argument about the video
- Provides strong and accurate details to support the argument about the video
- Considers other perspectives on the purpose and effectiveness of the video
- Makes connections between the video and the play
- Properly integrates quotations from the video
- Cites all sources used in the analysis

Time Period of the Play

Although Shakespeare wrote *Hamlet* around 1600, the story is set approximately 200 to 300 years earlier, when Europe was shifting from the Middle Ages to the Renaissance. At that time, European writers, artists, sculptors, and thinkers found a renewed interest in the great ancient societies of Rome and Greece. It was a shift from the Middle Ages, which occurred after the fall of Rome in 476 C.E. At that time, life was often harsh for peasants as they toiled in a **feudal** society.

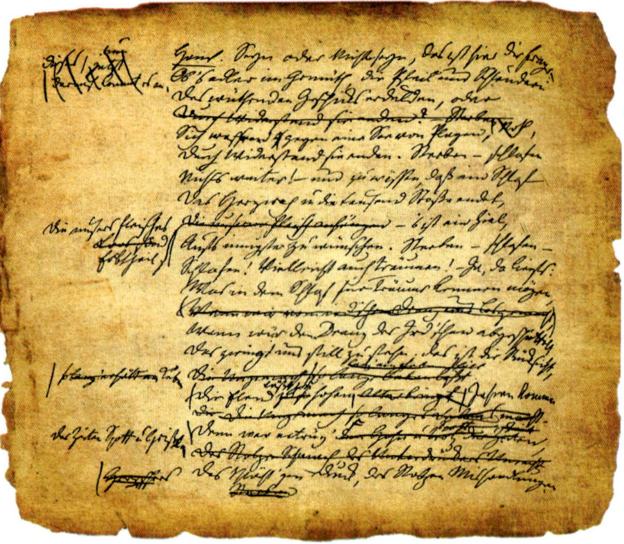

Hamlet

The Play's the Thing

Hamlet: "...Hum, I have heard
That guilty creatures, sitting at a play,
Have by the very cunning of the scene
Been struck so to the soul that presently
They have proclaim'd their malefactions.
For murder, though it have no tongue, will speak
With most miraculous organ. I'll have these players
Play something like the murder of my father
Before mine uncle. I'll observe his looks,
I'll tent him to the quick. If he but blench,
I know my course. The spirit that I have seen
May be the devil, and the devil hath power
To assume a pleasing shape, yea, and perhaps
Out of my weakness and my melancholy,
As he is very potent with such spirits,
Abuses me to damn me. I'll have grounds
More relative than this. The play's the thing
Wherein I'll catch the conscience of the King."

Hamlet, Act 2, Scene 2

Although the time period of the Renaissance varied from country to country, many historians consider it to have lasted from the fourteenth to the seventeenth century. The changeover marked the move to a more modern world. At the forefront of this change were writers and artists, such as Michelangelo and Leonardo da Vinci. Their artistic works were often funded by wealthy **patrons**. Their work and philosophies moved away from the religious underpinnings of the Middle Ages to more **humanist** traits.

Notable scientific discoveries were made during this time, as thinkers began to understand that Earth was not the center of the universe. The revolutionary printing press was invented by Johannes Gutenberg in the middle of the fifteenth century. Books, pamphlets, broadsides, and other printed materials were now available for mass consumption. The printing press changed how people thought about themselves and those who ruled them. New ideas about religion, politics, and culture moved quickly across the world.

People were also increasingly eager for plays. This desire can be seen in *Hamlet*, as Shakespeare adds a play to his play. Shakespeare uses the play within the play to provide Hamlet with a way to prove whether or not Claudius was instrumental in the king's death, as the ghost claimed.

ACTIVITIES

Video

Hamlet by William Shakespeare | Summary & Analysis

Discover some of the real-life events that may have inspired Shakespeare's *Hamlet* by watching this video.

1. In the video, Regina Buccola cites the tragic death of William Shakespeare's 11-year-old son, Hamnet, and the death of his father, John, as possible inspirations for *Hamlet*. What parallels can be drawn between these real-life events and the events of the play? Give textual evidence to support your answer.
2. How did the time period that *Hamlet* was written in impact Shakespeare's creation of the play? In what ways might the story be different if it were written today?

Weblink

The Influence of the Renaissance in Shakespeare's Time

Review the article by Lee Jamieson published on April 30, 2018.

1. In the article, Jamieson says that Shakespeare was a product of his time. How is the fact that Shakespeare was working in theater at the height of the Renaissance movement reflected in *Hamlet*? Give specific examples from the text.
2. Jamieson explains that Shakespeare "focused on creating human characters with psychological complexity," and cites *Hamlet* as the most famous example of this. In what ways does Hamlet exemplify this complexity? Which other characters from the play can be said to demonstrate this as well?

RUBRIC

Writing a Short Story

Students will choose an excerpt from the play and use it as their inspiration in writing a short story. An exemplary short story will meet the following criteria.

- Engages the reader from the opening line
- Establishes a clear, consistent point of view
- Introduces a narrator and a setting
- Develops an engaging conflict at the heart of the narrative to build tension and keep the reader interested
- Develops characters and events through purposeful and well-crafted literary devices
- Creates a logical progression of events in the narrative that build upon each other using various techniques
- Explores ideas, concepts, and writing styles with creativity and originality
- Demonstrates a high level of skill in using appropriate narrative techniques to tell the story
- Concludes the narrative in a thoughtful, effective manner appropriate to the narrative
- Uses varied, purposeful diction and syntax to affect style and serve the narrative
- Writes with clarity, imagination, and a unique, personal voice
- Does not use stereotypes or clichés
- Uses effective, believable dialogue
- Uses correct spelling, grammar, and punctuation

Conflict in the Play

Conflict in literature is a struggle between two or more opposing forces. When those forces clash, it creates tension that needs to be resolved. This struggle is often between the protagonist and antagonist, but there are other types of conflict found in literature. Without it, there is no story.

The Four Major Types of Conflict in Literature

MAN vs. MAN

A novel's protagonist struggles against an opposing character in a man versus man conflict. This opposing character is typically the book's antagonist, though this is not always the case. For instance, in *The Outsiders*, by S.E. Hinton, Ponyboy Curtis often clashes with his older brother, Darry, who is also his guardian.

MAN vs. SELF

A man versus self conflict occurs when a character's main struggle is internal. In *Holes*, by Louis Sachar, Stanley is sent to a boys' work camp as punishment for a crime he did not commit. The camp is a horrible place, with a vicious warden who mistreats the boys. In order to change his future, Stanley must believe in himself and champion the cause of the abused.

MAN vs. SOCIETY

A man versus society conflict is often based on the protagonist's beliefs. When a character does not agree with the beliefs or actions of a group, he or she may face challenges from society. This occurs in *The Help*, by Kathryn Stockett. Skeeter stands up to racism in her hometown of Jackson, Mississippi, in the 1960s. She collects stories from the town's maids to show how their employers mistreat them terribly.

MAN vs. NATURE

The protagonist is pitted against a natural obstacle in a man versus nature conflict. This can be an entire landscape, an animal, a natural disaster, or a symbolic representation of nature. In *The Road*, by Cormac McCarthy, an unnamed man and his son travel in a post-apocalyptic world and try to survive in a desolate land, facing many obstacles along the way.

Types of Conflict in *Hamlet*

The two main conflicts in *Hamlet* are man versus self and man versus man. Both of these conflicts have a major role in the play.

Man versus Self

Hamlet: "To be, or not to be, that is the question:
Whether 'tis nobler in the mind to suffer
The slings and arrows of outrageous fortune,
Or to take arms against a sea of troubles,
And by opposing end them. To die: to sleep;
...To sleep; perchance to dream. Ay, there's the rub;
For in that sleep of death what dreams may come,
When we have shuffled off this mortal coil..."

Hamlet, Act 3, Scene 1

Hamlet

Man versus Man

Hamlet: "Why, look you now, how unworthy a thing you make of me.
You would play upon me, you would seem to know my stops, you would pluck out the heart of my mystery, you would sound me from my lowest note to the top of my compass; and there is much music, excellent voice, in this little organ: yet cannot you make it speak. 'Sblood, do you think I am easier to be played on than a pipe? Call me what instrument you will, though you can fret me, yet you cannot play upon me."

Hamlet, Act 3, Scene 2

ACTIVITIES

More

The Types of Conflict in *Hamlet*
Analyze the excerpts from the play revealing the types of conflict as they appear in *Hamlet*.

1. How do these excerpts of conflict reveal the play's theme? How do they reveal character? Explain and defend your ideas.
2. Write an analysis of Shakespeare's development of conflict between Hamlet and Claudius. What deeper truths may be suggested about these characters as a result of their conflict?

Weblink

Elements of Drama: Conflict
Examine the blog post about conflict in theater.

1. What are the writer's goals and how does he attempt to accomplish them? How successful is he? Why do you think so?
2. Compare and contrast internal conflict with external conflict. In what ways are they similar? How do they differ? Give specific examples of each type of conflict. These can be from plays, novels, short stories, films, or television shows.

RUBRIC

Holding a Classroom Debate

Students will form groups and prepare arguments for a debate on a controversial issue. Exemplary performance in a debate will meet the following criteria.

- Demonstrates in-depth understanding of the topic and related information
- Presents strong, logical, and convincing arguments
- Communicates in a clear and confident manner
- Maintains eye contact
- Uses clear vocal tone and a reasonable rate of vocal delivery
- Uses respectful and appropriate language and body language
- Delivers arguments, evidence, and counter-evidence in an engaging and persuasive manner
- Supports each major point of an argument with several relevant and detailed facts and examples
- Connects all arguments to the overall topic in a clear, concise, and organized manner
- Presents the arguments and supporting evidence in a clear, logical manner
- Presents clear, thorough, and accurate information throughout the debate
- Addresses all of the opposing team's arguments with counter-arguments
- Identifies any weakness in the opposing team's arguments
- Constructs strong and relevant counter-arguments using accurate information
- Presents strong and persuasive arguments throughout the debate
- Summarizes the arguments in the closing statement

Introducing the Characters

Character development is central to the plot. Writers have several methods they use when giving life and depth to the people in their stories. The first is the direct method, when the audience sees the characters in action. The audience listens to their words, and understands what they are thinking and their motivations. The audience also watches their actions, including how they react with other characters. In *Hamlet*, much is revealed about the young prince through his **soliloquies**, and how he responds to his friends, family, and others.

Major Characters in *Hamlet*

Hamlet
Hamlet is the rightful heir to his father's throne. He seeks to avenge his father's death.

Gertrude
Gertrude loves her son, Hamlet, but is shallow and weak.

Claudius
Claudius is the king's brother and Hamlet's uncle. He is the play's main villain.

A playwright will also indirectly develop a character by having the audience see him or her through the eyes of others. Much is learned about Ophelia, for example, through her father, Polonius, her brother, Laertes, and Hamlet himself. Horatio also gives the audience a look into the mind of his friend, Hamlet.

Some characters are dynamic and help move the story forward. They change as the story unfolds. Hamlet is the most dynamic character in the play. He is a conflicted soul. Hamlet worries about the afterlife, the fate of his family, and his melancholy over the death of his father and the treachery that followed. He begins the play thinking one way, and completely changes his attitude by the play's end. Throughout, readers may wonder whether Hamlet is truly insane, or just acting mad as he seeks revenge.

Other characters are static. Polonius is a static character who never changes from scene to scene. Ophelia is also a static, one-dimensional character. Still others, such as Gertrude, Hamlet's mother, straddle the line between dynamic and static. Gertrude is a difficult person to characterize. She loves her son, but her motives are murky. Gertrude always plays it safe. She is charming, but shallow. Although she is graceful, Gertrude is also caught up in the trappings of wealth and power.

ACTIVITIES

Weblink

Character analysis: Gertrude in *Hamlet*

Review a character analysis of Gertrude and debate her role in the play.

1. As noted in the article, there is critical debate regarding Gertrude's role in the play. Is she simply a passive character or actually an insightful one? Explain your opinion of Gertrude and her importance in the play. Do you think she is a key figure? Give textual evidence to support your claims.
2. Tubb notes that there is much ambiguity surrounding Gertrude's character. In what ways can this be seen in the play? Do you think that Gertrude's loyalty is to her son, Hamlet, or to her new husband, Claudius?

More

Character Development in *Hamlet*

Analyze the characters in *Hamlet* using the descriptions on the character map and excerpts from each character. Then, choose a character and answer the following questions.

1. Which of the writer's techniques are most effective at revealing this character's traits? Why?
2. In what ways is the characterization of this character ineffective? What could be done to improve this character's function in the play? Defend your ideas with evidence.

RUBRIC

Creating a Literary Device Analysis Booklet

Students will analyze the author's use of a literary device in the play, and create a booklet to present this analysis. An exemplary literary device analysis booklet will meet the following criteria.

- Defines the chosen literary device accurately and in detail
- Places the definition of the literary device at the beginning of the booklet
- Provides strong, specific examples of how this literary device is used in the play
- Describes examples in detail, with quotations properly integrated
- Includes thorough analysis of the use, purpose, and effectiveness of each example of how the chosen literary device is used in the play
- Arranges all pages logically
- Examples are organized chronologically
- Provides no more than one example and its analysis per page
- Creates a neat, well-organized, and attractive booklet
- Booklet is colorful and displays the student's creativity
- Uses illustrations to represent the chosen literary device and the examples of how it is used in the play

The Art of Storytelling

Shakespeare is one of history's master storytellers. He wrote *Hamlet* during the Elizabethan Era, when England was ruled by Queen Elizabeth I. Shakespeare structured his plays by using different literary devices to create an overall message, including narrative and plot.

Structure of a Narrative

The narrative structure is something a writer must keep in mind when creating a story. The most common narrative structure is known as dramatic structure, or Freytag's Pyramid. The pyramid consists of five main components, which are all used in *Hamlet*.

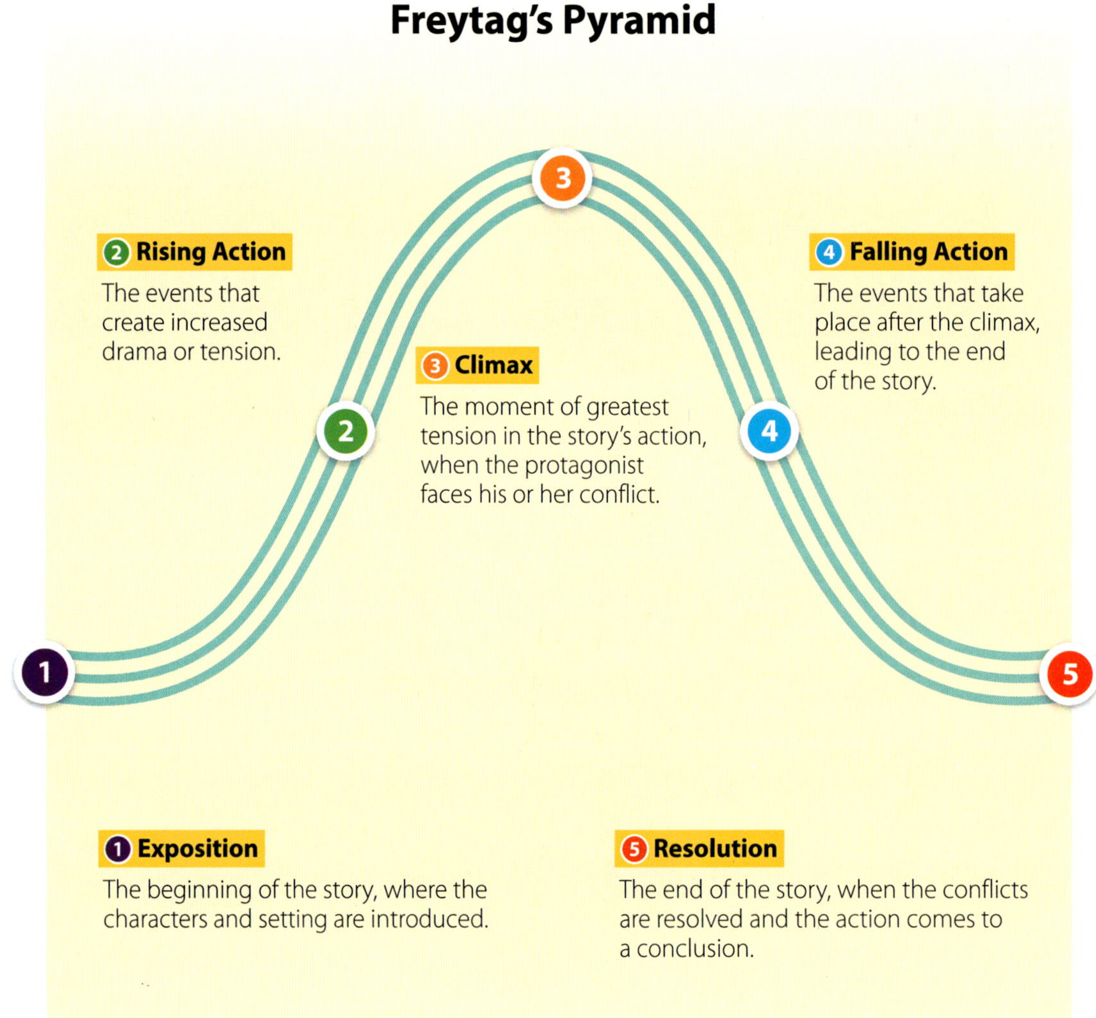

ACTIVITIES

Plot

Every play and novel has a plot, or events that move the story from one point to the next. The series in which these events take place is called the plotline. A well-organized plotline helps the narrative flow smoothly.

Plot Points in Act 1, Scene 1 of *Hamlet*

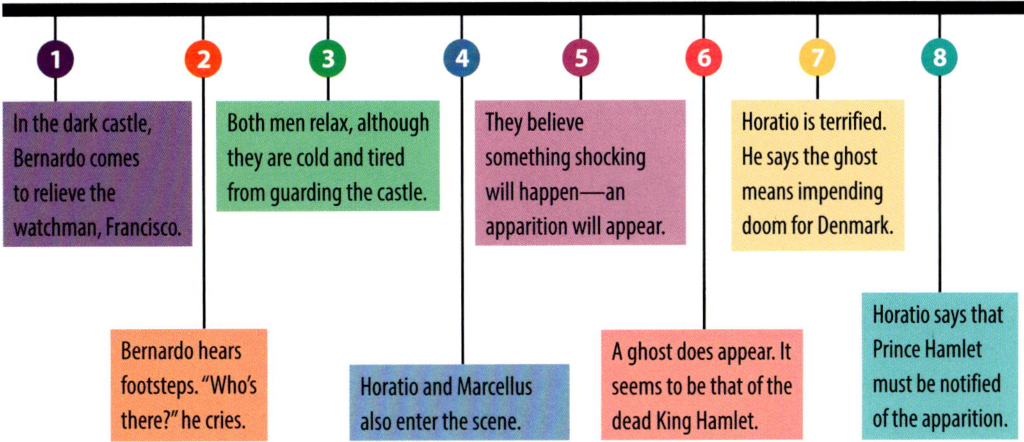

Literary Devices

A literary device is any feature of literature that can be identified, studied, and analyzed. Literary elements help make novels and plays interesting. Literary elements exist in every story. Literary techniques, however, vary depending on the writer's style, and the effect he or she wishes to achieve.

Video

Ophelia, Gertrude, and Regicide - Hamlet II: Crash Course Literature 204

Find out more about Hamlet's action and inaction in the play by watching this video.

1. In the video, John Green says that "taking action doesn't really resolve Hamlet's character" and that it is his "inaction, rather than his action, that makes us pay attention." What do you think he means by these assertions? Do you agree or disagree with John's claims? Support your answer with evidence from the play.
2. John wonders whether or not heroism always requires taking heroic action. What is your opinion on this topic? Why do you think Hamlet waits so long to take action? What are the results when he finally does? Explain whether or not his actions are heroic and why you think this is the case.

More

Examples of Literary Techniques from the Play

Analyze the author's use of literary techniques and how they contribute to the narrative of *Hamlet*.

1. Choose one literary technique used in the play. In what particular way did the author use this literary technique? How effective was its usage?
2. What arguments can be made for the use of your chosen literary technique in a text? If this technique were overused or underutilized, what effect might it have on an author's work?

Theme in the Play

The theme of a story is a general, universal statement, or main idea. Often times, themes are evident and stated outright. Other times, themes are insinuated, so the reader can make his or her own judgments. Plays and novels can have multiple themes, although one is typically stronger than the others. Theme should not be confused with the play's topic, or overall subject. Themes can be expressed as events, dialogue, or actions. One reader might have a different interpretation of a theme than another.

Values

It is impossible to identify a play's themes without considering the values of each character. Values are what a person believes. They are what drives the characters' behavior. Each character in *Hamlet* has different values. Gertrude wants to keep her station in life. Claudius will do anything to retain power. Polonius will do anything to remain in the king's favor. Theatergoers or readers can gain a sense of the characters' values through their words and actions. Values often play a large role in the story's conflict. Characters with differing values are juxtaposed with each other and help to reveal the theme of the play or novel. Characters with evolving values can also help to highlight aspects of a play's theme.

Major Themes of *Hamlet*

Revenge is the overarching theme of *Hamlet*. Hamlet is urged by his ghostly father to seek revenge on the new king, Claudius, who killed him. Laertes also seeks to avenge his father's death, at the hands of Hamlet.

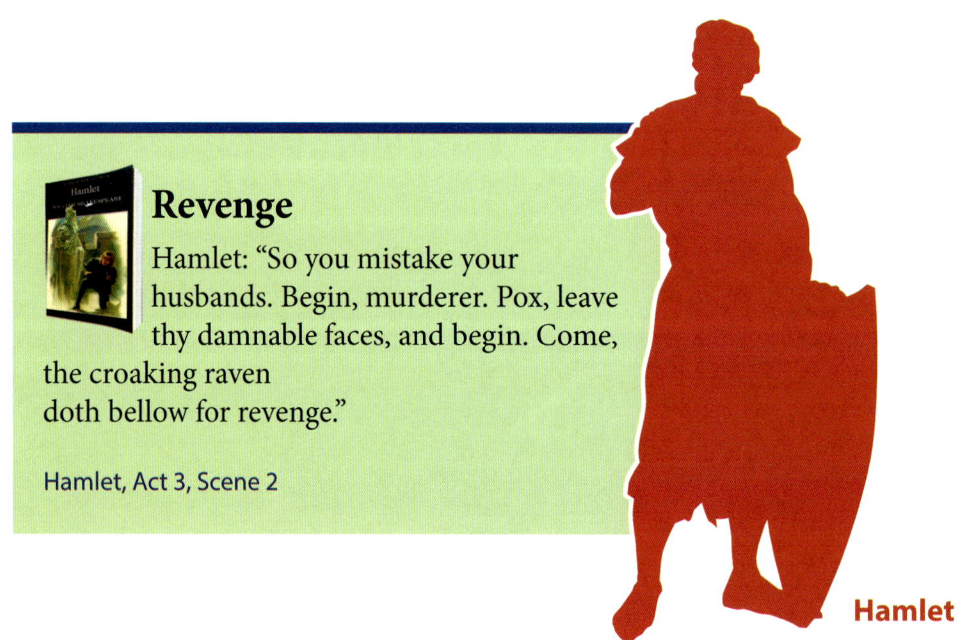

Revenge

Hamlet: "So you mistake your husbands. Begin, murderer. Pox, leave thy damnable faces, and begin. Come, the croaking raven doth bellow for revenge."

Hamlet, Act 3, Scene 2

Hamlet

ACTIVITIES

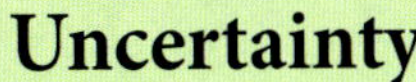

Uncertainty

Hamlet: "Get thee to a nunnery. Why wouldst thou be a breeder of sinners? I am myself indifferent honest, but yet I could accuse me of such things that it were better my mother had not borne me. I am very proud, revengeful, **ambitious**, with more offences at my beck than I have thoughts to put them in, imagination to give them shape, or time to act them in. What should such fellows as I do crawling between heaven and earth? We are arrant knaves all. Believe none of us. Go thy ways to a nunnery..."

Hamlet, Act 3, Scene 1

Death

Hamlet: "...Alexander died,
Alexander was buried, Alexander returneth into dust, the dust is earth, of earth we make loam, and why of that loam, whereto he was converted, might they not stop a beer-barrel?
Imperious Caesar, dead and turn'd to clay,
Might stop a hole to keep the wind away..."

Hamlet, Act 5, Scene 1

Hamlet

Secondary Themes

Uncertainty and death are secondary themes. For most of the play, Hamlet does not react. He needs to be certain, but that certainty is fraught with emotional, ethical, and psychological minefields. When he does act, Hamlet moves haphazardly, recklessly, and without thinking. An example of this is when he murders Polonius. Hamlet is also obsessed with the idea of death, and even considers his own demise. He ponders spiritual questions, not only when he sees his dead father's ghost, but also when he sees the remains of others.

Weblink

***Hamlet* and revenge**
Evaluate the article discussing revenge in the play.

1. The writer of the article, Kiernan Ryan, states that *Hamlet* is a deliberate attempt by Shakespeare to sabotage the revenge tragedy genre. Analyze the arguments he makes to support this position. How effective are they? Do you agree with his examples or might they be interpreted in another way? Explain your answer.
2. It has often been said by critics that Hamlet's retribution comes too late. Do you think this is true? Could any of the deaths that occur in the play have been prevented had Hamlet exacted his revenge on Claudius sooner? Why or why not?

More

Major and Secondary Themes
Analyze the author's development of themes over the course of the play.

1. Choose a secondary theme from this spread and analyze its appearances in the play. How does this theme first emerge? Which is the most poignant example of this theme in the play?
2. What particular commentary might the author be making about life as a result of this theme's presence in the text? Explain and defend your ideas.
3. Choose a major theme presented on pages 16–17. In what ways does your chosen secondary theme relate to this major theme? Does it deepen or detract from the major theme? How or in what way?

RUBRIC

Creating a Symbolism Poster

Students will choose one of the other symbols listed on page 19 and analyze its role in the play. They will then create a poster to present their analysis. An exemplary symbolism poster will meet the following criteria.

- Presents a clear purpose that is conveyed throughout the poster
- Shows an understanding of the concept of symbolism and the role it has in the play
- Provides an in-depth analysis of what the symbol represents
- Discusses the role the symbol has in the play
- Clearly indicates where the symbol appears in the play
- Uses specific, detailed examples from the text to support the analysis
- Makes clear connections to the text
- Properly integrates all quotations
- Organizes the information in a logical, easy-to-read manner
- Includes high-quality graphics that relate to the symbol and effectively enhance understanding of the topic
- Features clear and concise writing
- Uses correct spelling, grammar, and punctuation
- Clearly labels items of importance
- Headings and subheadings are clear and easy to read
- Uses layout to creatively enhances the information
- Creates a poster that is attractive in terms of layout, design, and organization
- Shows a strong effort by the student

Symbolism in the Play

Writers use symbolism as a technique to help the reader understand the themes of the story. A symbol is often an object that can be seen and touched. Writers use particular objects to impart a deeper meaning. Symbols can reveal a writer's feelings about a specific idea or concept. By identifying and analyzing the symbols a writer uses, the reader can gain a deeper understanding of the story.

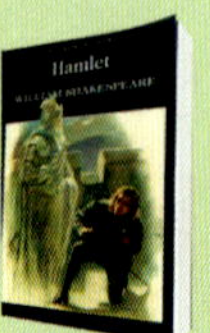

Poison

Ghost: "...Upon my secure hour thy uncle stole,
With juice of cursed hebenon in a vial,
And in the porches of my ears did pour
The leperous distilment; whose effect
Holds such an enmity with blood of man
That swift as quicksilver it courses through
The natural gates and alleys of the body,
And with a sudden vigour it doth posset
And curd, like eager droppings into milk,
The thin and wholesome blood. So did it mine;
And a most instant tetter bark'd about,
Most lazar-like, with vile and loathsome crust,
All my smooth body..."

Ghost to Hamlet, Act 1, Scene 5

Poison

In *Hamlet*, poison is a symbol of dishonesty, disloyalty, death, treachery, and **corruption**. Claudius uses poison to kill his brother, the king, which then allows him to marry the king's wife. When Laertes learns that Hamlet has killed Polonius, Claudius convinces him to avenge his father's death by dueling Hamlet with a sword dabbed with poison. To ensure Hamlet's death should the prince win the duel, Claudius also poisons a cup of wine, which he plans to give to Hamlet.

There are two main ways Shakespeare uses poison in *Hamlet*. Poison is used in a figurative sense, when Hamlet describes the marriage of his uncle to his mother as poisonous to the family. Shakespeare also uses "poison" when the actors are performing *The Murder of Gonzago*, by having them pour poison in the king's ear, which is how Hamlet suspects that Claudius killed his father. Shakespeare uses "poison" as a pun, but one that has a deeper meaning.

Where Does Poison Appear in the Play?

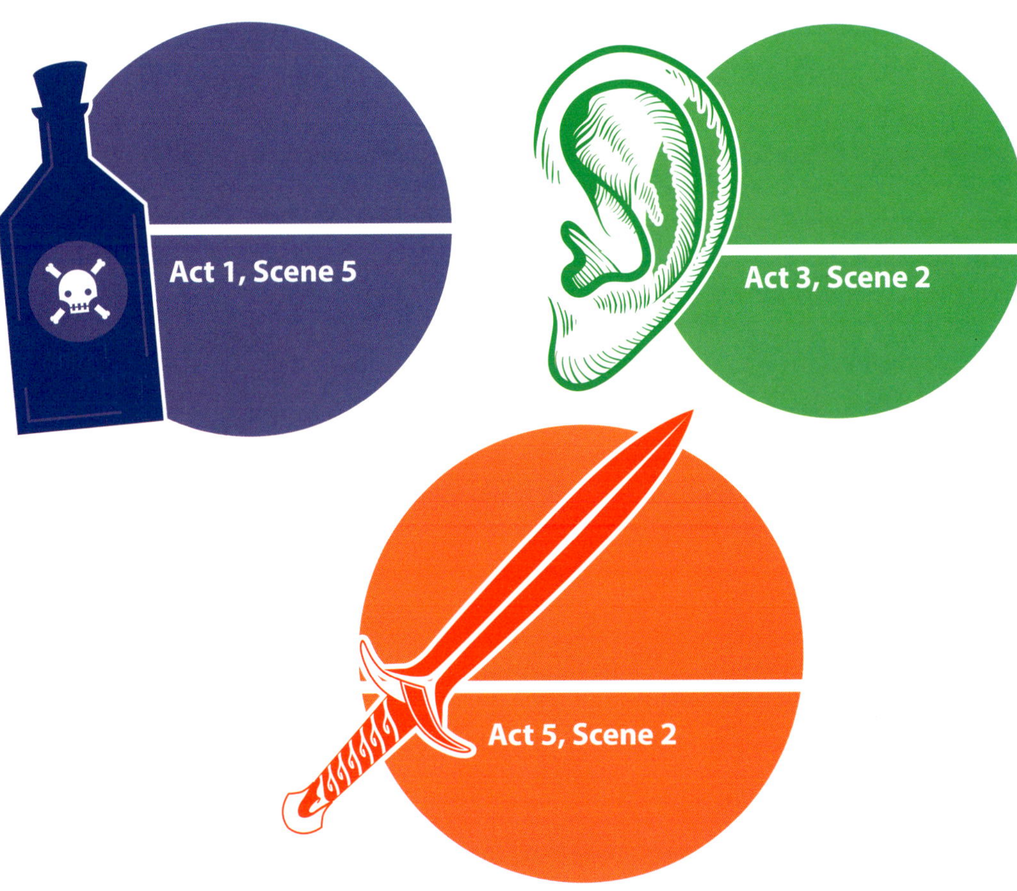

Other Symbols in the Play

Yorick's Skull

When Hamlet discovers Yorick's skull in the grave, he speaks directly to it. The skull symbolizes the inevitability of death. It also symbolizes the body's ultimate destruction.

The Ghost

The ghost of king Hamlet is another symbol of the inevitability of death. Yet, the ghost is also immortal, and represents the haunting memories of reality. In Shakespeare's time, writers often used ghosts in their revenge tales.

Hamlet's Clothes

Hamlet wears all black, a symbol of mourning, which irritates his mother. In fact, Hamlet seems to be the only person in the castle mourning his father's death. His clothes are in direct contrast to those of Gertrude and Claudius, who want everyone to forget the king's death. His "suits of solemn black," cannot adequately describe what Hamlet is feeling inside.

ACTIVITIES

 **More**

What Symbols Appear in the Play?
Assess the author's use of symbolism in the play.

1. Choose a scene from the chart and analyze what this excerpt represents. For which character is poison the most poignant symbol in the play? For which character is it least poignant? Argue your opinions with clear reasons.
2. How is poison used or reflected in the play's themes? Illustrate the ways in which the author's use of language deepens or weakens the meaning of this symbol. Explain and defend your ideas.

Weblink

The Complete Guide to Symbolism
Examine the blog post discussing the usage of symbolism in literature.

1. Contrast and compare examples of analytical descriptions of feelings and sensory descriptions using symbolism from the play. Which kind is more effective in the play? Provide reasons for your ideas.
2. Should analytical descriptions play a considerable role in the language of a play? Why or why not?

The Use of Language

Writers use language like a surgeon uses a scalpel—it is the most important tool they have, especially for playwrights whose words are spoken rather than read. The language of Shakespeare may seem odd by today's standards, and sometimes impossible to understand. Yet, it is rich and has many layers. When Shakespeare started out as a writer, the English language was brimming with new words, as English speakers traveled the world trading and exploring other countries. Shakespeare himself created new words and expressions that are still in use today. Phrases such as, "a fool's paradise," "forgone conclusion," and "star-crossed lovers," are just a handful of examples.

Figurative language is often defined as the way an author uses various descriptive techniques to create dramatic, poetic, or descriptive effects. It is the opposite of literal language, which is language that means exactly what it says. Figurative language uses similes, metaphors, puns, allusion, and imagery. Shakespeare was a master of figurative language.

Puns

A pun is the use of wordplay, in which words that sound alike are traded by characters, usually for humorous effect. Shakespeare is known for using puns, not only in *Hamlet*, but also in his other plays. There are many puns exchanged between Claudius and Hamlet in Act 1, Scene 2 of *Hamlet*. In these few lines, Claudius asks Hamlet why he is still depressed. Hamlet uses the word "Sun," a play on the word "son," because he believes he is the son of too many people—his mother, his dead father, and now his stepfather, Claudius.

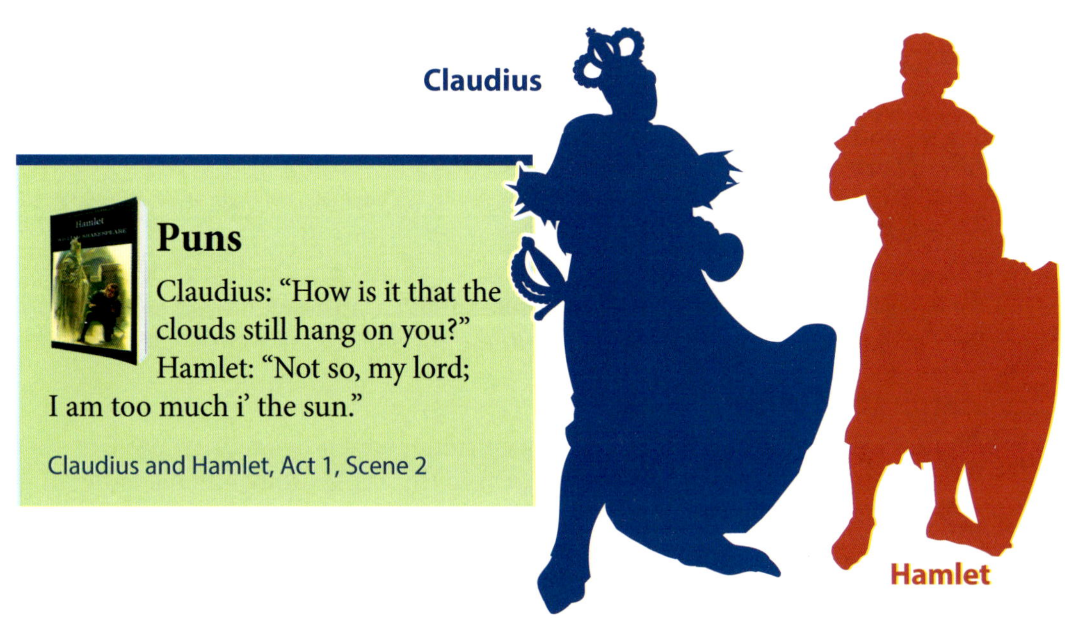

Puns

Claudius: "How is it that the clouds still hang on you?"
Hamlet: "Not so, my lord;
I am too much i' the sun."

Claudius and Hamlet, Act 1, Scene 2

Turn of Phrase

Shakespeare loved to invent phrases, many of which can be found in *Hamlet*. These phrases have become everyday utterances for many people. In fact, they have been used so many times that some have become trite.

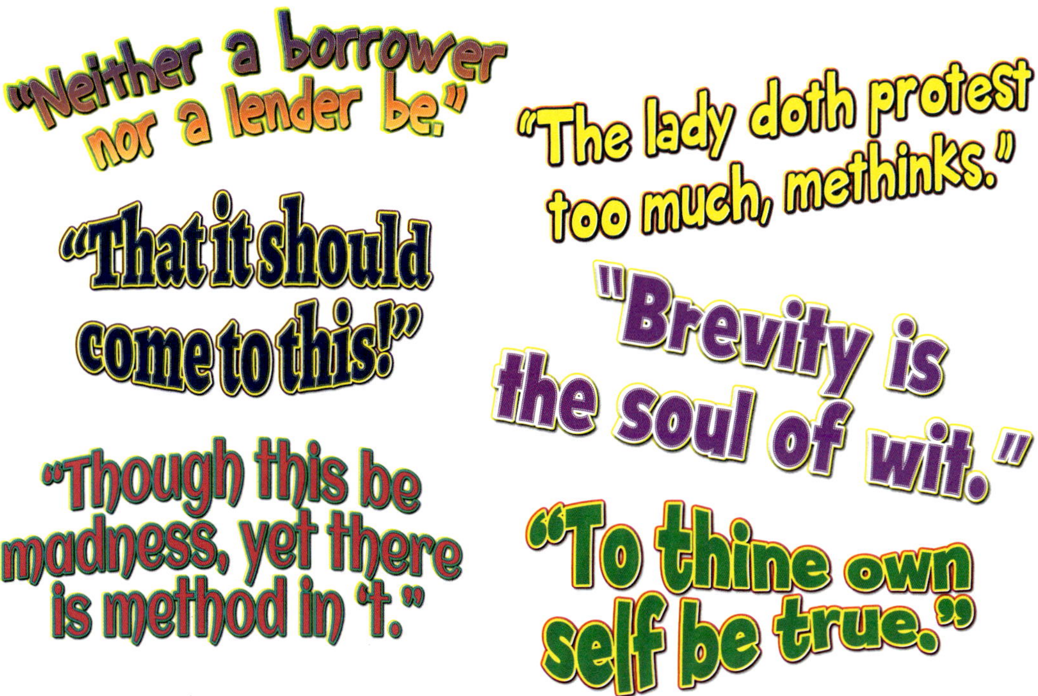

Iambic Pentameter

Shakespeare divided his verse into meters, whether a line rhymed or not. Specifically, his characters speak in iambic pentameter. An "iamb" is an unaccented syllable, followed by an accented syllable. For example, the word revenge could be broken down into iambic pentameter as "re/venge," with the accent on the second syllable.

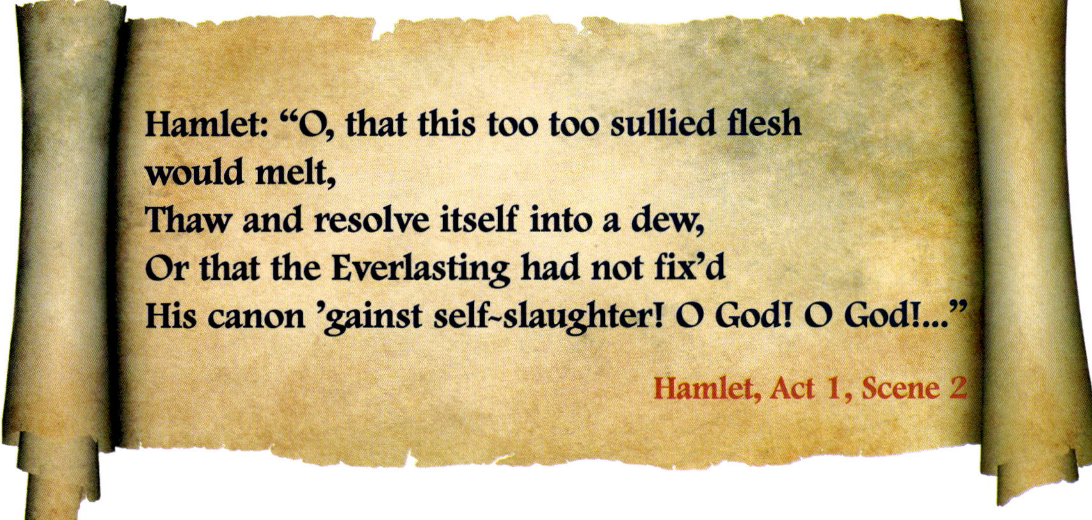

ACTIVITIES

Document

Shakespeare's Language Strategies in *Hamlet*
Review the *Journal of Literature and Art Studies* article by Mufeed Al-Abdullah and Susanne Ramadan.

1. Who do you think is the intended audience for this document? Why? Are the tone and language used appropriate for this audience? Explain your answer.
2. What are the main points of the document and how are they presented? Are these points conveyed effectively to the reader? Why or why not?

Weblink

Hamlet's Puns and Paradoxes
Explore some of the puns made by Hamlet in the play.

1. Why does a melancholy character such as Hamlet make so many puns throughout the play? How does this affect the way he is perceived by the audience?
2. What effects do Hamlet's puns have on his interactions with the other characters in the play? Explain your answer.

RUBRIC

Writing a Review

Students will write a review of the play. An exemplary review will meet the following criteria.

- Grabs the reader's attention with a creative headline
- Begins with an engaging lead to pull the reader into the article
- Introduces the title of the play, the author, and the genre
- Provides a brief plot description that does not give away the entire story, and makes the reader want to learn more about the play
- Supports arguments about the play with accurate and detailed information
- Organizes the review and its arguments in a concise, clear, and logical manner
- Fits the format and style of a review
- Follows the conventions of print or online journalism
- Demonstrates creativity in their approach
- Writes with a unique, engaging voice and perspective
- Provides fresh insight into the play
- Provides an honest, authentic opinion on the play
- Gives a clear recommendation on the play, backed up by specific textual evidence
- Uses correct spelling, grammar, and punctuation

Impact of the Play When First Performed

For many scholars, *Hamlet* was the first great tragedy that had been produced in Europe since the works of Greece two thousand years earlier. Why Shakespeare wrote it, like much of his life, remains a mystery. Scholars agree that the story has its origins in Norse legend. Hamlet resembles Amlethus, a figure found in *The History of the Danes*, which was penned around 1200. One scholar, Dr. Lisa Collinson, believes that the origin of Hamlet's name is medieval Gaelic from a story called *The Destruction of Da Derga's Hostel*, which was written one hundred years earlier, based on material dating to the eighth and ninth centuries.

The famed Globe Theatre opened in 1599. Shakespeare was an investor in the theatre, and shared in its profits, along with other members of the Lord Chamberlain's Men acting troupe. It is believed that Shakespeare designed *Hamlet*, along with several of his other plays, for performance at the Globe. Although there are no official records, historians think that *Hamlet* was first performed at the Globe in 1600 or 1601.

Ocean-Going Performance

Hamlet's first recorded performance at sea was in 1607, on a ship called the *Red Dragon*. The ship was sitting off the coast of Sierra Leone, West Africa, at the time. The captain of the ship, which was owned by the East Indian Company, wrote in his journal that the play kept, "my people from idleness and unlawful games, or sleep."

ACTIVITIES

One of the First Princes

One of the first actors to play Hamlet was Thomas Betterton, in 1661. At that time, Betterton was in his 20s, and played the young prince for another 50 or so years. He told his audiences that he was still, "a young man of great expectation, vivacity, and enterprise," when he was in his 70s. Throughout the years, Shakespeare's original text had been shortened. Long speeches were cut, and risqué references to the mad Ophelia were sliced.

Acting Hamlet

In the 1700s, audiences were enthralled by David Garrick's interpretation of Hamlet. Garrick was so convincing that he trembled and shook when the ghost appeared. His knees knocked together, his mouth stood agape, and his hat fell off. His performance was so realistic that friends feared Garrick would fall to the ground.

At **age 29, Ethan Hawke** was the **youngest** modern actor to play Hamlet **on film**. **Ben Wishaw**'s performance at **age 23** makes him the **youngest** actor ever to play Hamlet **on stage**.

Sir Johnston Forbes-Roberts became the **oldest** actor to play Hamlet **on film** at **age 60** in **1913**.

There are **183 rhyming lines** in Hamlet.

Document

First Quarto of Hamlet

Compare the first published version of *Hamlet* with the version you have studied by viewing the first quarto.

1. The first quarto, often called Q1, was printed in 1603, about three years after the first performances of the play. How is Hamlet presented differently in Q1 from the way he appears in later versions? In what ways is he similar? What do you think may account for these variations?
2. How might reading this version of *Hamlet* change the way you experience the play? Why?

Weblink

How one actor forever changed the way we see Shakespeare

Find out more about David Garrick's influence on our opinions of Shakespeare in this *British Council* article by Richard Schoch, published on April 19, 2016.

1. According to Schoch, Garrick is responsible for forming "the popular attitudes towards Shakespeare that remain to this day." What attitudes is he referring to, and why does he believe this to be the case?
2. Schoch claims that Garrick was "the single most important figure in 18th century Shakespeare." Do you agree with this assertion? Why or why not?

Impact of the Play Now

Despite being written more than 400 years ago, *Hamlet* is still one of the most imitated and relevant plays of the modern era. Its themes of revenge, power, lust, and intrigue continue to resonate. The play has been made into several motion pictures and television adaptations over the years.

The Lion King

The Lion King, Disney's popular animated movie, is loosely based on *Hamlet*. It features the death of King Mufasa at the hands, or claws, of his scheming brother, Scar. The king's son, Simba, is visited by his father's ghost. The movie, however, which is targeted to children, has a vastly different ending than Shakespeare's play.

1966 Christopher Plummer was nominated for an Emmy in 1966 for his portrayal of Hamlet.

In **1949**, **Laurence Olivier** became the only actor to ever win an **Academy Award** for playing Hamlet.

The **longest-running Broadway performance** of *Hamlet* was **137 shows** in **1964**. **Richard Burton** played the title role.

Kenneth Branagh's *Hamlet*

Many critics consider Kenneth Branagh's 1996 film adaptation of *Hamlet* as one of the best of the modern era. Branagh sought to bring Shakespeare to a new and younger audience, not only with *Hamlet* but also in his film version of the Shakespearean comedy, *Much Ado About Nothing*. *The New York Times* said of *Hamlet* and Branagh, "As star and ringmaster, Mr. Branagh gets to the heart of '*Hamlet*' and goes to admirable lengths to take his audience there, too."

On the Modern Stage

Actor John Gielgud played Hamlet more than 500 times on the stage in New York, London, and at Elsinore in Denmark. Critics have often called him the definitive Hamlet. Although Gielgud died in 2000, others have taken on the role, adding their own interpretations to the brooding son of a dead king. In 2017, the Public Theater in New York City put on its interpretation, with Oscar Isaac in the title role. In the words of *The New York Times*, the play, directed by Sam Gold, "treats Shakespeare's daunting tragedy with an easy, jokey familiarity... [T]he creative team here obviously knows and loves its Hamlet so very well."

Hamlet Meets Bart Simpson

The popular cartoon, *The Simpsons*, also paid homage to *Hamlet*, as Homer, the patriarch of the clan, reads the play to two of his children. "Once upon a time, there was a young prince of Denmark," Homer begins. The show then segues into a dreamlike state in which Bart is Hamlet and Homer is the king's ghost.

ACTIVITIES

Weblink

Why is Hamlet more relevant than ever?

Evaluate the article discussing why *Hamlet* still matters today.

1. In the article, Harry Daniels debates *Hamlet*'s place in modern society. What reasons does he give to refute critics who have written off Shakespeare's works as outdated or contrived? Assess both arguments, explaining which side you support and why.
2. Daniels claims that Hamlet demonstrates the connection between people. Do you think he is correct? Why or why not?

Document

Hamlet review – Maxine Peake is a delicately ferocious Prince of Denmark

Analyze the review by Susannah Clapp, published on September 21, 2014, exploring her views on Maxine Peake's performance as Hamlet.

1. Although the role of Hamlet is often performed by a male actor, Clapp points out that many women have also performed the role over the years, dating as far back as the late 1700s. Why does Hamlet work so well as a role for both men and women? How does the performer's gender affect the audience's interpretation of the play, if at all?
2. Clapp says that "The speeches that come out of the prince's mouth are about dissolving, yet the person who delivers them has to be the most distinct, intense character on stage." Why do you think this is the case? What qualities must the actors portraying the other characters display, in contrast to Hamlet?

RUBRIC

Creating a Timeline

Students will explore a topic related to the play and create a timeline to present their research on historical events connected to this topic. An exemplary timeline will meet the following criteria.

- Includes the most significant events pertaining to the topic to be compared and analyzed
- Includes interesting events
- Uses accurate information for all events, including date, location, and major details
- Orders the events in a chronological sequence
- Describes each event with accurate, vivid, and specific details
- Presents the topic from three or more perspectives
- Inspires the reader to ask thoughtful questions regarding the events and perspectives presented in the timeline
- Uses correct spelling, grammar, and punctuation
- Presents the timeline in a visually attractive and striking manner
- Presents the timeline in a neat, organized manner that is logical and easy to follow
- Uses creativity to present the timeline in an engaging manner
- Effectively communicates the historical information relating to the topic
- Supports each event with reliable sources
- Expresses a clear purpose for creating the timeline
- Enhances the reader's understanding of the topic
- Includes a correctly formatted bibliography of all sources used to create the timeline

Perspectives on the Future of a Nation

While *Hamlet* brims with a variety of themes, there is another leitmotif that is also part of the play—that of a nation in turmoil. *Hamlet* was relevant when it was first produced. At the time *Hamlet* first appeared on stage, questions swirled about who would succeed the aging **monarch**, Queen Elizabeth I. Audiences could understand the tension of the play, as Spain had tried to invade England, and there was an attempt to assassinate Queen Elizabeth I.

Timeline of Murdered Monarchs

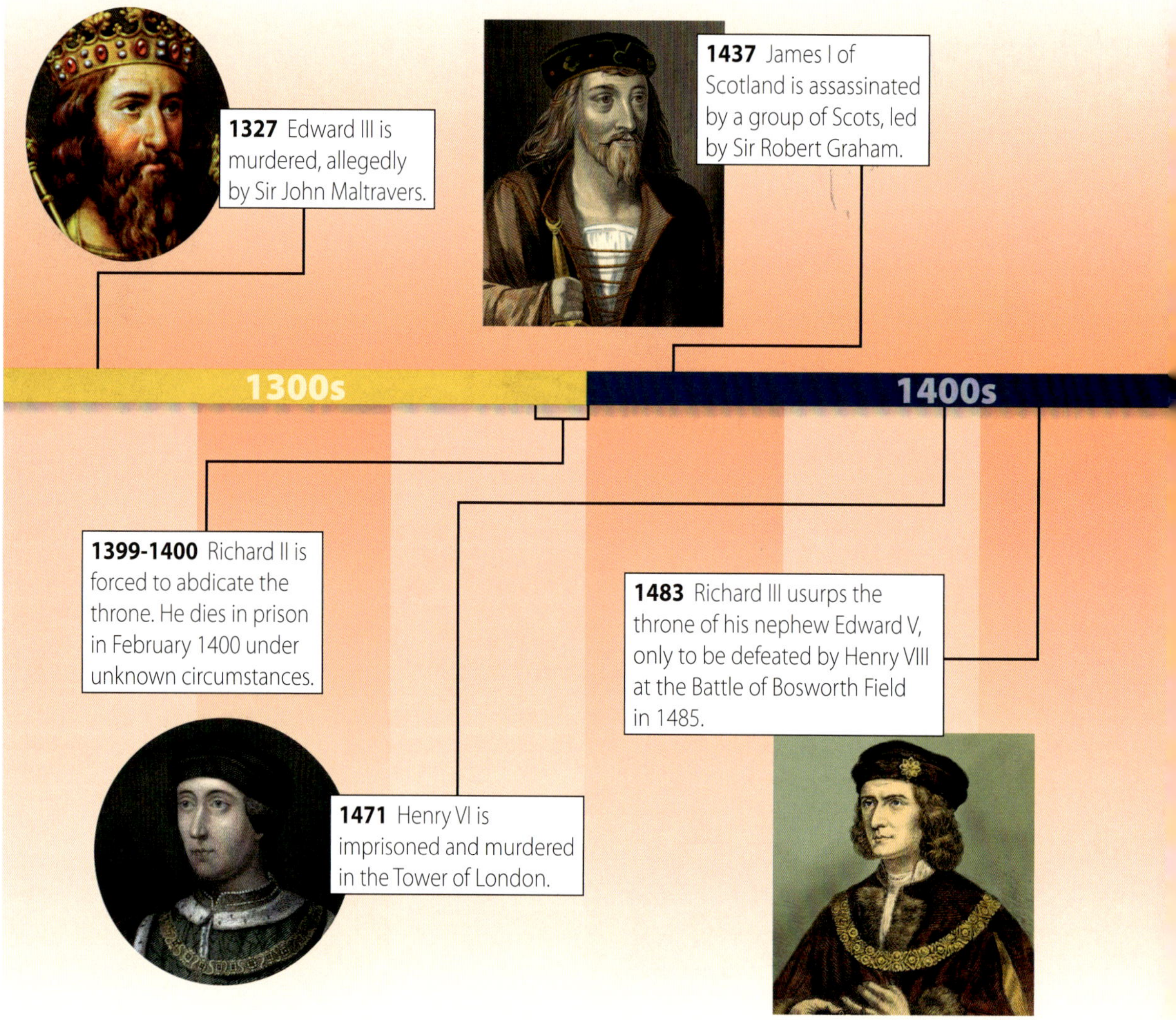

1300s

1327 Edward III is murdered, allegedly by Sir John Maltravers.

1399-1400 Richard II is forced to abdicate the throne. He dies in prison in February 1400 under unknown circumstances.

1400s

1437 James I of Scotland is assassinated by a group of Scots, led by Sir Robert Graham.

1471 Henry VI is imprisoned and murdered in the Tower of London.

1483 Richard III usurps the throne of his nephew Edward V, only to be defeated by Henry VIII at the Battle of Bosworth Field in 1485.

Hamlet also explores the anxiety that surrounds power and succession. The first indication of a wounded nation appears early in Act 1, when the audience finds out that Claudius has poisoned Hamlet's father, the rightful king of Denmark, and ascended to the throne. Theatergoers slowly begin to understand that Denmark itself is a sickly body, corrupted by Claudius, Gertrude, Polonius, and others. In fact, the well-known line, "[s]omething is rotten in the state of Denmark," is a not-so-subtle sign that the soul of the country is poisoned, much like many of the play's characters. This break of the natural line of succession would likely have resonated with audiences who were concerned about the real-life succession of Queen Elizabeth I.

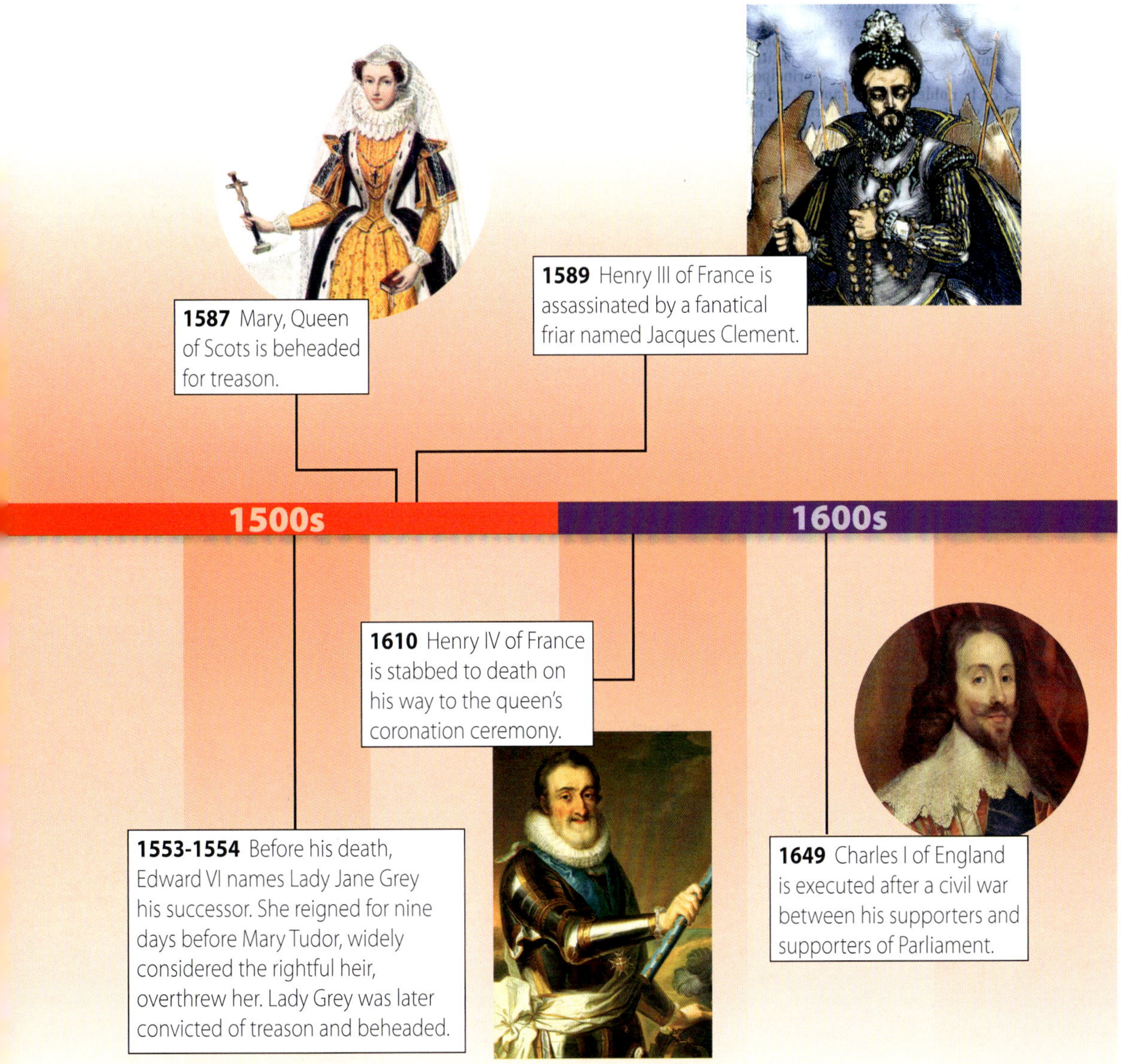

1587 Mary, Queen of Scots is beheaded for treason.

1589 Henry III of France is assassinated by a fanatical friar named Jacques Clement.

1500s

1600s

1610 Henry IV of France is stabbed to death on his way to the queen's coronation ceremony.

1553-1554 Before his death, Edward VI names Lady Jane Grey his successor. She reigned for nine days before Mary Tudor, widely considered the rightful heir, overthrew her. Lady Grey was later convicted of treason and beheaded.

1649 Charles I of England is executed after a civil war between his supporters and supporters of Parliament.

ACTIVITIES

Transparency–Timeline

Timeline of Murdered Monarchs

Examine the historical and cultural contexts shown on the timeline. Then, contrast and correlate its elements with the themes and events presented in *Hamlet.*

1. In what ways can historical events, culture, and social mores influence a population's perspective on a monarchy? How might these elements have shaped the way a viewer in the 1600s interpreted the play?
2. How might the era in which William Shakespeare wrote *Hamlet* have influenced the play's themes and settings? Where in the play is this most evident? Explain your reasoning.
3. Which current events, changes in laws, new ideas, or political discussions are shaping people's perspective of the British monarchy today? Which ideas and attitudes are still prevailing? Why?
4. How might current events and present perspectives affect the way a reader interprets the play? Why is it important for readers to understand the era and context in which a play is written?

RUBRIC

Writing a Comparative Essay

Students will compare two literary devices used in the play, and then write a comparative essay based on their analysis. An exemplary comparative essay will meet the following criteria.

- Consists of a one-paragraph introduction, three body paragraphs, and a one-paragraph conclusion
- Introduction includes an engaging lead statement about the topic of the essay, more detailed information about the play, and a one-sentence thesis that specifically states the essay's argument
- Body paragraphs include a topic sentence that refers to the thesis and how the idea appears in the play, a supporting sentence that points to this part of the play, textual evidence of this idea from the play, and analysis of this evidence
- Body paragraphs end with a transition to the next paragraph
- Conclusion refers to the topic of the essay and the three points presented in the body paragraphs, and restates the thesis
- Provides a thorough analysis of the literary devices in question
- Cites strong and thorough textual evidence to support analysis of what the play says explicitly
- Presents a clear, specific thesis that indicates a high level of critical engagement
- Organizes ideas in a logical manner
- Communicates arguments in a clear, effective manner
- Properly integrates all quotations
- Correctly cites all sources used
- Correctly formats bibliography

Writing a Comparative Essay

Hamlet brings together many interesting characters and themes that still resonate today. Once you are done reading, write a comparative essay to explore how Shakespeare uses two literary devices to move the play forward. This could be a comparison of characters, themes, symbols, or settings. To write a comparative essay, you will need to formulate an argument. Your argument should clearly state how you feel your compared elements are similar or different. Support your argument with sufficient evidence from the play and valid reasoning.

How to Analyze and Compare Characters

Use the chart to guide your comparison of two characters in *Hamlet*.

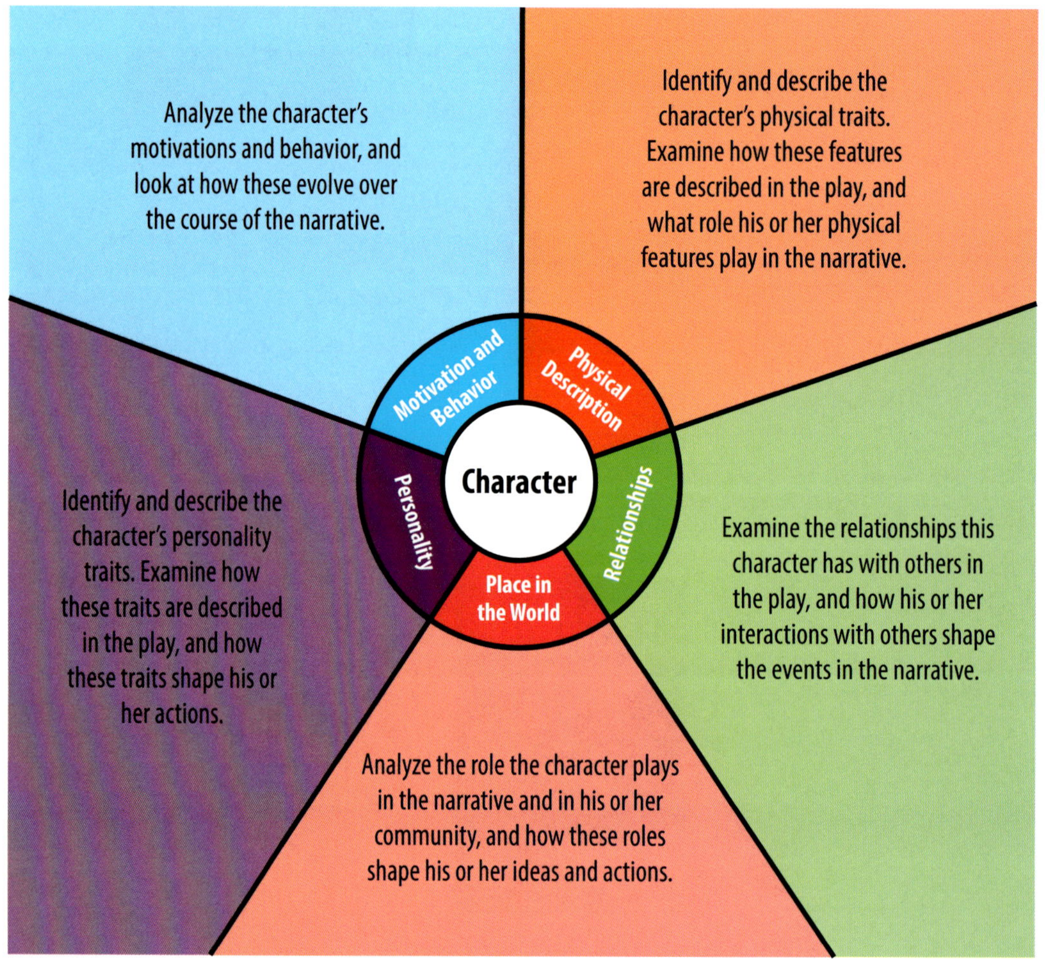

ACTIVITIES

Comparing Hamlet and Claudius

Hamlet

Relationships
- Son to Gertrude and King Hamlet
- Nephew to Claudius
- Friend to Horatio

Place in the World
- Protagonist
- Prince
- Should have been the rightful heir to the throne

Motivation and Behavior
- Is obsessed with his father's death
- Vengeful
- Behaves rashly and impulsively
- Is motivated by the intrigue between his mother and Claudius
- Upsets other characters with wild innuendos
- Purposely turns everyone against him

Personality
- Always says there is more to him than meets the eye
- Brooding
- Maudlin
- Cunning
- Deceitful
- Philosophical
- Contemplative
- Makes everyone think he is insane

Physical Description
- Young
- Always wears black
- Always melancholy

Claudius

Physical Description
- Older

Motivation and Behavior
- Wants to hold on to power
- Crafty
- Does not want others to know he killed the king
- Works to gain people's trust
- Ambitious
- Unapologetic
- Takes responsibility for his actions, to a point

Place in the World
- Antagonist
- King

Relationships
- Brother to King Hamlet
- King of Denmark
- Husband to Gertrude
- Uncle to Hamlet

Personality
- Conniving
- Shrewd
- Lustful
- Manipulative
- Preoccupied with himself
- Charming

More

Questions for Character Analysis

Analyze how specific character features, such as conflicts, motivations, relationships, place in the world, and personality affect the plot of *Hamlet*. Cite strong and thorough textual evidence to support your analysis of what the play says explicitly as well as the inferences you may have drawn from the play's setting, themes, and symbols.

Quiz Answers

1. A
2. B
3. C
4. A
5. C
6. C
7. A
8. C
9. C
10. D

Key Words

ambitious: having a desire for success or power

corruption: dishonest and disloyal conduct

dispensation: exemption from a rule or requirement

feudal: political and economic system where tenant farmers pay landlords for the right to farm their land

humanist: during the Renaissance, those who studied ancient Greek and Roman culture that emphasized critical individual thought

monarch: a person, such as a king, queen, or emperor, who rules over a country or kingdom

patrons: during the Renaissance, those who gave financial support to artists and writers

proverbs: stories that state a general truth

shareholder: person who owns stock in a company

soliloquies: speeches where a person speaks one's thoughts aloud

Literary Terms

action: everything that occurs in a narrative

antagonist: the character who stands in opposition to the protagonist; in some cases, the antagonist creates or represents the conflict that the protagonist faces

characterization: the act of describing a character through the person's appearance and personality

climax: the moment of greatest tension in the story's action

conflict: a struggle between two or more opposing forces, creating tension that must be resolved

dialogue: the words spoken between characters in a story

exposition: the beginning of the story, where the characters and setting are introduced

falling action: the events that take place after the climax, leading up to the end of the story

foil: in literature, a character who contrasts with another character

Freytag's Pyramid: a narrative structure consisting of five elements; this includes exposition, rising action, climax, falling action, and resolution

hyperbole: an exaggerated statement

leitmotif: a recurrent theme associated with a particular person, idea, or situation

literary elements: components of every literary work

literary techniques: unique structures of a literary work

metaphor: figure of speech in which a writer compares two different things without using a word of comparison such as like or as

narrative: a logically arranged series of events presented for an audience; a story

plot: the specific action that propels a story forward

protagonist: the central character in a piece of fiction who must deal with a conflict and often undergoes some type of change as a result

resolution: the end of the story, when the problems are resolved

rising action: the events that create increased drama or tension

simile: figure of speech that compares the similarities between two different objects using words such as like or as

style: the unique way that writers use language to tell their stories; this can include word choice, the use of imagery, and the length and organization

symbolism: a stylistic device using symbols to represent and intensify concepts and ideas

theme: the underlying topic, idea, or position in a work that is often a general, universal statement

Index

LIGHTBOX

SUPPLEMENTARY RESOURCES

Click on the plus icon found in the bottom left corner of each spread to open additional teacher resources.

- Download and print the book's quizzes and activities
- Access curriculum correlations
- Explore additional web applications that enhance the Lightbox experience

LIGHTBOX DIGITAL TITLES

Packed full of integrated media

VIDEOS

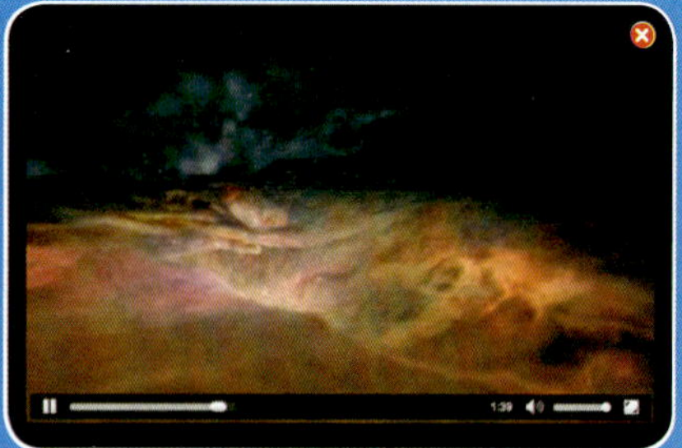

INTERACTIVE MAPS

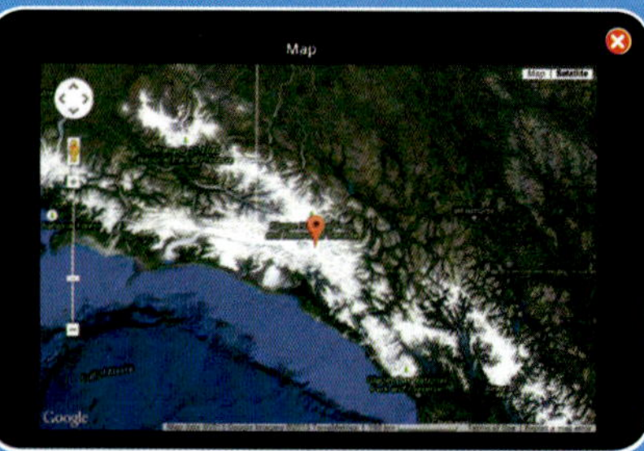

WEBLINKS

SLIDESHOWS

QUIZZES

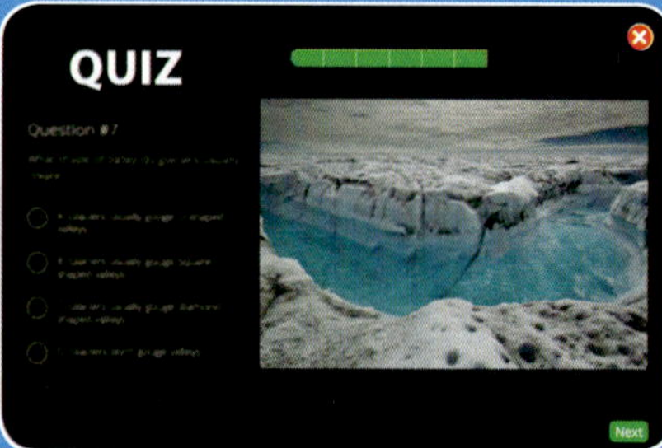

OPTIMIZED FOR

- ✓ TABLETS
- ✓ WHITEBOARDS
- ✓ COMPUTERS
- ✓ AND MUCH MORE!

Published by Smartbook Media Inc.
350 5th Avenue, 59th Floor New York, NY 10118
Website: www.openlightbox.com

Library of Congress Cataloging-in-Publication Data
Names: Perritano, John, author. | Gillespie, Katie, author.
Title: Hamlet / John Perritano and Katie Gillespie.
Description: New York, NY : Smartbook Media Inc., 2018. | Series: Lightbox literature studies | Includes index.
Identifiers: LCCN 2017054096 (print) | LCCN 2018004600 (ebook) | ISBN 9781510536975 (Multi-User eBook) | ISBN 9781510536968 (hard cover : alk.paper)
Subjects: LCSH: Shakespeare, William, 1564-1616. Hamlet--History and criticism. | Shakespeare, William, 1564-1616. Hamlet--Examinations--Study guides. | Hamlet (Legendary character) | Fathers in literature. | Murderin literature. | Revenge in literature. | Denmark--In literature.
Classification: LCC PR2807 (ebook) | LCC PR2807 .P375 2018 (print) | DDC 822.3/3--dc23
LC record available at https://lccn.loc.gov/2017054096

Printed in Brainerd, Minnesota, United States
1 2 3 4 5 6 7 8 9 0 22 21 20 19 18

062018
121017

Editor: Katie Gillespie
Art Director: Terry Paulhus

The publisher acknowledges Getty Images, iStock, Alamy, and Shutterstock as its primary image suppliers for this title.